Omni
Learning
Center

GUIDE TO READING COMPREHENSION STRATEGIES

An OMNI LEARNING CENTER Educational Guide

LORRAINE GERSTL

GUIDE TO READING COMPREHENSION STRATEGIES
An OMNI LEARNING CENTER Educational Guide

ISBN 978-1-950134-26-7
OMNI LEARNING CENTER EDUCATIONAL GUIDES
an Imprint of PANGÆA PUBLISHING GROUP

Lorraine Gerstl cover photo by Marc Howard

Cover & interior design and typesetting by
DesignPeaks@gmail.com

DESIGN PEAKS©

The books are available at special quantity discounts for bulk purchase.
For details, write to: *sales@OmniLearningCenter.org*

The book is available at special quantity discounts for bulk purchase.
For details, write to: *sales@OmniLearningCenter.org*

Omni Learning Center

25579 Carmel Knolls Drive, Carmel - CA, 93923
Telephone: 831-277-3387 / 831-224-0742
contact@OmniLearningCenter.org
www.OmniLearningCenter.org

To

Greg, Karen, Roslyn, Jeff & Tracy
and
to the readers of today
who will become the leaders of tomorrow
Oliver, Fineas, Vivian
Jake, Abby & Ryland

and always for my Hugo

ACKNOWLEDGMENTS

I gratefully thank and appreciate the editorial support and assistance of Connie St. Amour, Margaret Klompas, Harry Klompas, Linda Elliott, and my Omni partner and dear friend, Margaret Lotz, and the brilliant design work, cover, interior and guidance of Lisa Peaks.

TABLE OF CONTENTS

INTRODUCTION

"I know I should read more, but I'm so busy, it takes *time* to read, and so much of what I try to read doesn't really make that much sense to me ..." Those can be the words of a third grader or, just as easily, the words of an adult. In our hurry-up world of bits and bytes, and the need for instant gratification, the sad and simple truth is that people don't read as much as they used to and, more tragic, they understand what they read far less than in the past.

In this practical, hands-on Guide, the author, a Master Teacher with more than thirty-five years of practical success teaching both children and adults of all ages, shares her ideas on teaching reading comprehension strategies! The underlying message she delivers is: **Comprehensive Strategies are important because Reading is an <u>Active</u>, not a Passive, Process.**

Reading can seem incredibly complicated. It involves not only making sense of the squiggles on a page – deciphering the alphabetic code and figuring out the words, but reading also entails giving meaning to, understanding, and thereby *enjoying* what we read.

Reading comprehension is absolutely critical to communication, whether it involves a doctor healing a patient, a lawyer presenting an argument in court, an astronaut needing to know how to repair a malfunction when he is thousands of miles above the earth, or, most important, enriching and widening the scope of your life! In fact you cannot think of one area of learning or practice where understanding what you read is not absolutely essential.

The more you *understand* what you read, the less of a drudgery and the more of a joy it becomes. *Reading is the key that unlocks the door to the universe.*

In this book, I teach you the underlying *secrets* I've gleaned from *decades* of successfully watching as students of all ages glow when they first discover the wonder of, "I can *understand* it and I can *do* it – and I never thought I could!"

Get ready to start a great adventure – and to grab hold of the key that will unlock the door to *your* universe!

PRE-READING ACTIVITIES

What is done *before* reading is extremely beneficial for students to understand text. This preparation work is what helps students connect new information to what they already know.

Sample pre-reading activities may include:

- Examining the pictures and captions to learn more about what the text is going to say.
- Asking students what they know about the topic.
- Looking at the subtitles and asking students to consider anything they know about them.
- Checking the graphs and maps to discover how they might add meaning to the text.
- Looking at the boldface words.
- Asking students to write a question they anticipate will be answered in the text.
- Discussing new vocabulary and trying to attach it to something students already know.

SOME GOOD PROBES TO USE BEFORE YOUR CHILD STARTS TO READ

- What do you think this text will be about?
- What would you like to know about _____?
- What does this (text feature) make you wonder about?
- What are some questions you expect the author to answer?
- Why do you suppose the author chose _____ for the title of the text?
- What questions could you ask just from the title alone?
- Why do you think the illustrator used the feature she or he did in this picture?
- How does this picture make you feel? Why?
- Do the subtitles seem to fit within the major title? Do any of them surprise you and/or make you wonder about something?

PROBES TO USE LATER IN THE TEXT

- What do you think will happen now? What makes you think so?
- What further questions would you ask the author if you could?
- What would you ask the main character if she or he stepped out of the book right now?

FIRST STRATEGY – SCHEMA AND CONNECTIONS

SCHEMA: WHAT YOU ALREADY KNOW AND HAVE IN YOUR BRAIN

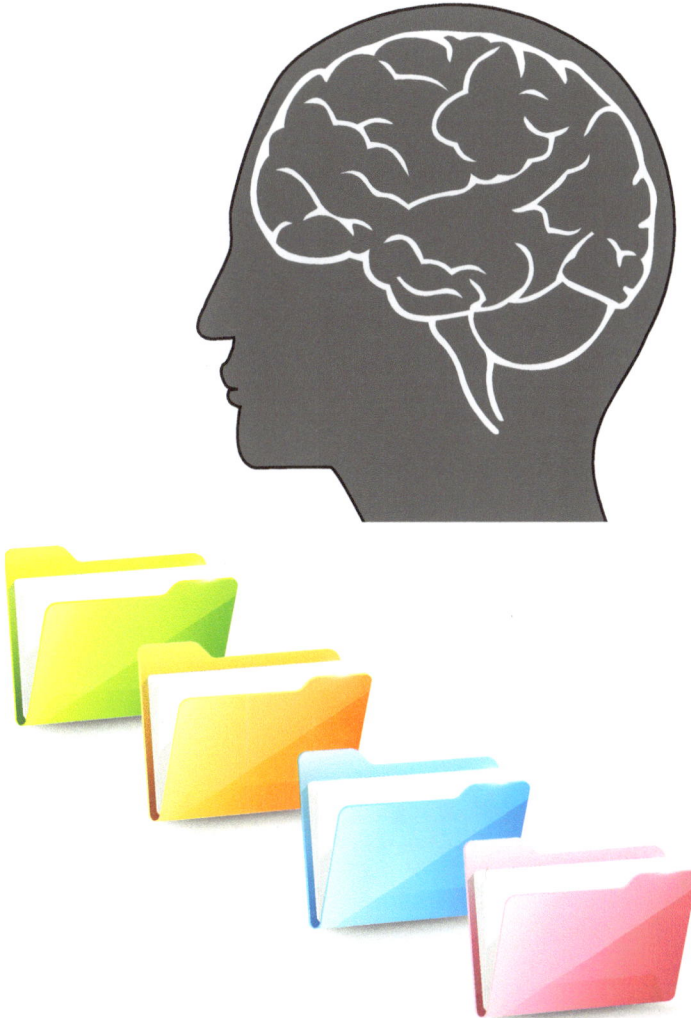

Our **schema** is like our personal mental filing cabinet. It contains all the information we have in our brains. Within our "filing cabinet" we have "folders" holding all our *known* information. There may be a "folder" for books we have read, for sports, for movies, one about pets, our recipes, and games we play. **As we read and learn, we connect new information to the existing information in our brains.**

SUGGESTED ACTIVITIES

To introduce Schema to students, pretend you are inviting them to your home for a party. Even though they have never been to your home, their schema - the knowledge in their mental filing cabinet - will help them think about what they may see in your home – a living room with furniture, books, bedrooms, bathrooms, a kitchen, birthday treats, a pet, etc.

To brainstorm on a topic and activate schema, students can use Concept Webs. This is especially useful when reading nonfiction.

Concept Web

The concept web, which is ideal for brainstorming, helps you activate your schema on a topic you are reading about. Write the topic of your book (or a vocabulary word from the book) in the center circle. Use the web extensions, or file folders from your schema to show what you know about the topic.

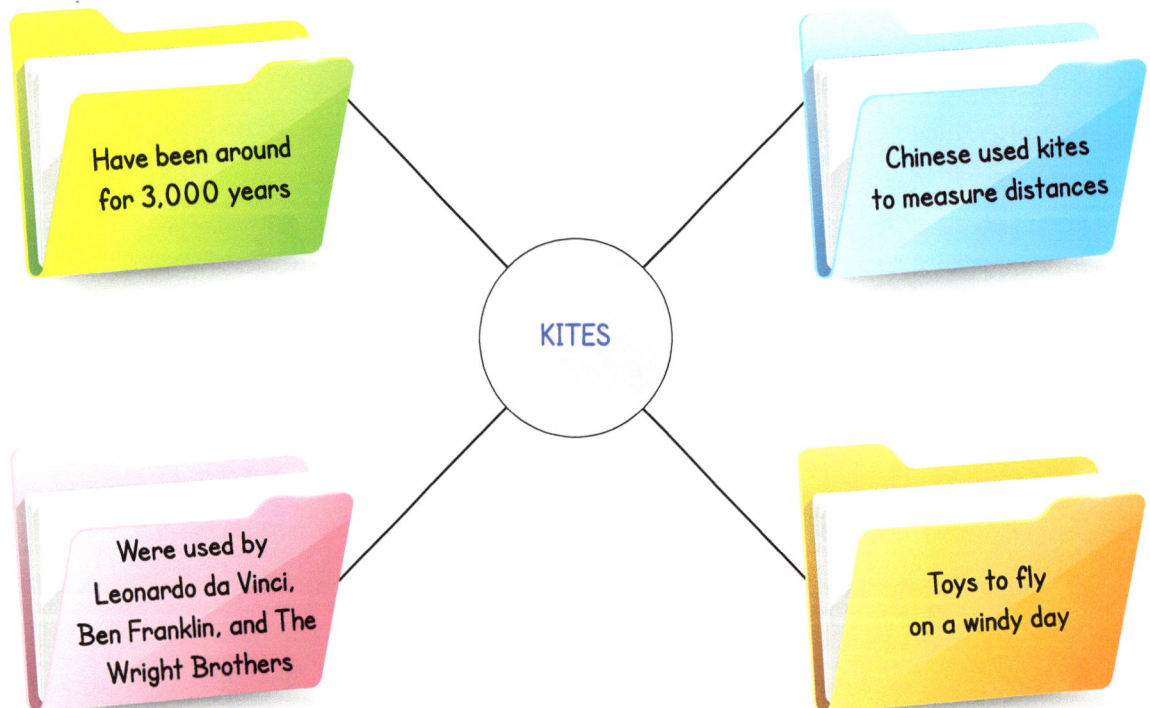

Have been around for 3,000 years

Chinese used kites to measure distances

KITES

Were used by Leonardo da Vinci, Ben Franklin, and The Wright Brothers

Toys to fly on a windy day

MAKING CONNECTIONS:

There are *three ways* to make connections between existing knowledge and newly acquired information. I have included charts to help students record their connections. It is important for them to record on these charts how these connections have helped their understanding of what they are reading, supported by evidence from the text.

1. *Text-to-Self Connections* - make a connection to your personal life.

Connection Stems students may want to use:

- This reminds me of…
- I remember a time when…
- I have had a similar experience to…
- I know how the character feels because…
- How is this different from anything that has ever happened to me?
- Do I know a person like the main character in the story?
- Have I visited any place like the setting in the story?

Text to Self   TEXT-TO-SELF CONNECTIONS CHART

Title: *Wemberly Worried* by Kevin Henkes

MY TEXT-TO-SELF CONNECTION	HELPED ME UNDERSTAND BECAUSE
"Wemberly worried about everything." P.1	Wemberly reminds me of myself, because I worry about everything. I feel I understand Wemberly.
"On her birthday, Wemberly worried that no one would come to her party." P.12	When I give a party, I always worry that everything may not turn out well.
"Wemberly had a new worry: school." P.17	I understand. I worry that each day may not be special for our students.

2. *Text-to-Text Connections* - make a connection to another book.

Connection Stems students may want to use:

- How is this book similar to other books I have read?
- How is it different from other books I have read?
- Do the characters remind me of characters in another book?
- Does the setting remind me of settings in other books

Text to Text

TEXT-TO-TEXT CONNECTIONS CHART

Title: *Wanted Dead or Alive: The True Story of Harriet Tubman* by Ann McGovern

MY TEXT-TO-TEXT CONNECTION	HELPED ME UNDERSTAND BECAUSE
Reading *Wanted Dead or Alive: The True Story of Harriet Tubman*, made me think of another text called *If You Traveled on the Underground Railroad*.	*If you Traveled on The Underground Railroad*, gave me a lot of background information, and many examples of runaway slaves and how they were treated. So I was able to sympathize with Harriet Tubman and it made it easier for me to understand how badly she felt and how difficult her life was.

3. *Text-to-world Connections* - make a connection to an event happening in the world.

Connection Stems students may want to use:

- Does this remind me of something happening in the outside world now?
- Are there links in the news to this?
- Has someone else mentioned something about this to you?

Text to World   **TEXT-TO-WORLD CONNECTIONS CHART**

Title: *Malala, A Brave Girl from Pakistan*
by Jeanette Winter

MY TEXT-TO-WORLD CONNECTION	HELPED ME UNDERSTAND BECAUSE
When I read this book, it reminded me of articles I have read and television news I have seen about girls who are discriminated against and who are unable to receive the same educational opportunities as boys.	I felt I could understand Malala's situation more clearly; that despite violence against her, she would not give up her fight for equal rights for all people.

Books to use to teach Schema and Making Connections

- *Chrysanthemum* by Kevin Henkes
- *Wemberly Worried* by Kevin Henkes
- *Alexander and the Terrible Horrible No Good Very Bad Day* by Judith Viorst
- *Chicken Sunday* by Patricia Polacco
- *The Keeping Quilt* by Patricia Polacco
- *Come on Rain* by Karen Hesse
- *Lightning* by Seymour Simon
- *The Wall* by Eve Bunting
- *My Great Aunt Arizona* by Gloria Houston

SECOND STRATEGY – PREDICTION

A **prediction** is an educated guess that can be confirmed or disaffirmed through further reading. Predicting actively engages students with the text by asking them what they think may occur in the rest of the story. Predictions are created by combining two things: (1) clues the author leaves for the reader (words, pictures, or text features); and

(2) activation of their schema. As students find evidence to form speculations, they also ask questions, recall facts, reread, infer, draw conclusions, and, ultimately, comprehend the text more fully. It is important that children understand that their predictions must be **supported by evidence from the text**. Help students think about where the evidence came from by asking such questions as, "What made you say that?" or "Can you find an example from the text or pictures?"

SUGGESTED ACTIVITIES

Play a simple game in which students will be required to support their predictions with evidence.

- Put the kettle on to boil. Put a tea bag in a mug.
  What do students predict is going to happen next?
- Pick up a book, put on reading glasses, and settle down in a chair.
  Stop and ask your students to predict what you are going to do next.

Ask them in both cases to provide observations or clues that support their predictions.

Books to use to teach Predicting:

- *Two Bad Ants* by Chris Van Allsburg
- *Strega Nona* by Tomie de Paola
- *A River Ran Wild* by Lynn Cherry
- *Wednesday Surprise* by Eve Bunting
- *The Day Gogo Went to Vote* by Sisulu
- *I'm in Charge of Celebrations* by Byrd Baylor
- *Amazing Grace* by Mary Hoffman

THIRD STRATEGY – VISUALIZATION

Good readers use the strategy of **visualization** to help them make pictures in their minds, based on what they already know and understand about the world around them. They access their schema, make connections, predict and infer information. The mental images readers make are unique to them. When students visualize, they use all of their senses to help them imagine or picture something in their minds.

Most of all, visualizing helps students to develop the habit of *actively thinking* about what they read.

SUGGESTED ACTIVITIES

One way to introduce the idea of visualizing is to have students listen to a piece of music and then draw the mental images or the story the music tells.

Some of the music pieces I've used to introduce this strategy were:

- *The Flight of the Bumblebee* by Rimsky-Korsakov
- *1812 Overture* by Tchaikovsky
- *Rondo Alla Turca* by Mozart
- *The Sting Theme* by Scott Joplin
- *Pomp and Circumstance* by Edward Elgar

Another way to help students visualize is to suggest they think of an event or experience they have enjoyed, and then have them draw the mental image they see in their minds.

Books to use to teach Visualizing:

- *A Chair for Mother* by Vera B. Williams
- *Eleanor* by Barbara Cooney
- *Owl Moon* by Jane Yolen.
- *Where the Wild Things Are* by Maurice Sendak
- *Song and Dance Man* by Karen Ackerman
- *I'm in Charge of Celebrations* by Byrd Baylor
- *A Bad Case of the Stripes* by David Shannon

FOURTH STRATEGY – CHARACTERIZATION

Character traits are aspects of a person's behavior. They are often labeled with descriptive adjectives. Readers determine what characters are like by what they say and what they do, and how the author or illustrator portrays them.

To help students identify character traits teach them this acronym: F.A.S.T. for Feelings, Actions, Sayings and Thoughts.

F.A.S.T: FEELINGS - ACTIONS - SAYINGS - THOUGHTS

In the boxes below, describe the Feelings, Actions, Sayings and Thoughts of your character.

Title: *Junkyard Wonders* by Patricia Polacco
Character's Name: Patricia

FEELINGS	ACTIONS
She felt like the odd man out, because the normal kids would not hang around with her, laughed at her, and made her feel different and not accepted.	Patricia was sad and cried at home, but she slowly discovered she could make friends with people who were truly worthwhile and who had a bigger spirit than the so called "popular kids."

SAYINGS	THOUGHTS
"Oh daddy, I have been put in a special class again. It is called The Junkyard."	Patricia thought that all of the tribes made worthwhile projects, but that her tribe's plane was the best.

Characters may also be described by both their outward appearance and by their inner personality traits. After showing an example of an Inner/Outward Character Trait Poster, have students create either a Character Poster of themselves , or one of someone they know very well. The Inner/Outward poster should contain at least five traits under each heading.

INSIDE/OUTSIDE CHARACTER TRAIT

Title of the Book: *A Bad Case of the Stripes*
Author: David Shannon
Character's Name: Camilla

OUTSIDE: Appearance What does the character look like on the outside?	INSIDE: Character Traits What is the character like on the inside?
Very colorful	Sad
Covered in multi-colored stripes	Trying to fit in
Black hair	Very nervous
Has a pink bow	Really scared
Black eyes	Loves lima beans, but is afraid to admit it

Authors give their characters certain traits to help them come alive.

A Character Map may help a student recognize and analyze characters.

CHARACTER MAP

Title of the Book: *A New Coat for Anna*
Author: Harriet Ziefert

How the Character Acts and Feels.	How Others Think About this Character.
Anna is very patient, very appreciative, and friendly.	The other characters seem to like Anna and want to help her. She makes them feel happy.

Character's Name
Anna

Describe the Character's Outward Appearance.	What Does the Character Like or Dislike?
Anna is a cute, loving little girl with chubby rosy cheeks and brown hair.	She likes the sheep and watching all steps that are involved in making a coat. She is also happy to participate as she watches the coat take shape.

OPEN-MIND PORTRAITS

To help students think more deeply about a character and reflect on the events of the story from a character's point of view, or to show the development of a character, students may want to draw an open-mind portrait of that character. These portraits have at least two parts. The face of the character is on one page, and the mind of the character is on the following pages. Here are the steps to making an open-mind portrait:

- Draw and color a portrait of the head of the character you are describing.
- Cut out the portrait and trace around it to make as many other pages of the head as you need. These mind pages will reflect what the character is thinking or how the character is feeling at various points in the story.
- Staple the pages together in order with the portrait on the top.
- Students can lift the portrait and then draw or write about the character from the character's point of view on the successive mind pages.

Books to use to teach Characterization

- *A Bad Case of the Stripes* by David Shannon
- *The Librarian of Basra* by Jeanette Winter
- *Thank you Mr. Faulkner* by Patricia Polacco
- *My Rotten Red-Headed Older Brother* by Patricia Polacco
- *The Junkyard Wonders* by Patrica Polacco
- *Mufaro's Beautiful Daughters* by John L. Steptoe
- *The Stranger* by Chris Van Allsburg
- *Eleanor, Quiet no More: The Life of Eleanor Roosevelt* by Doreen Rappaport

FIFTH STRATEGY – RETELLING AND STORY MAPPING

Retelling a story allows students to organize and describe events in sequence, which enhances their reading comprehension. It is a strategy that readers use to think about what they are reading. Good readers stop and retell the text to help them understand the story.

Students need to understand the *difference between retelling and summarizing*.

- A **summary** is direct and to the point. It is like a postcard of a vacation. Summarizing is recounting the story with just the important events.
- A **retelling** is the entire scrapbook. It provides as many details as possible and is usually an oral activity. In retelling, we use specific details, such as the characters' names, and the setting. Instead of, "She went to the store," say, "Julie went to the Pet Store after school."

If students cannot retell a story, they probably did not fully understand it.

In order to retell a story, it is important to know the Elements of a Story and how to make Story Maps.

BASIC ELEMENTS OF A STORY

CHARACTERS (who?)	People or animals who move the story forward
SETTING (where? when?)	Place, time, season
PROBLEM (Conflict, Challenge)	Every story worth its salt has a problem. No problem, no story!
PLOT (what?)	The main events in the story
RESOLUTION (how?)	How the problem is resolved
THEME (The Message)	(not included in a retelling)

RETELLING GUIDE

The title of the story is . . .	Grandma and the Pirates by Phoebe Gilman
The characters are . . .	Grandma, Melissa, Oliver, and three pirates
The story takes place . . .	In a little house in a meadow by the ocean
In the beginning . . .	Grandma puts a pudding out to cool on the windowsill
Then . . .	The pirates steal the pudding, and kidnap Grandma and Oliver
After that . . .	Melissa is stolen by the pirates while trying to save Grandma and Oliver
And then . . .	Melissa, Grandma, and Oliver try to escape
Then . . .	Melissa tricks the pirates and steals their ship
In the end . . .	Melissa, Grandma, and Oliver cleverly abandon the pirates and sail home.

Students may enjoy retelling their stories in puzzle form.

STORY ELEMENTS

The Parts that make up a Story

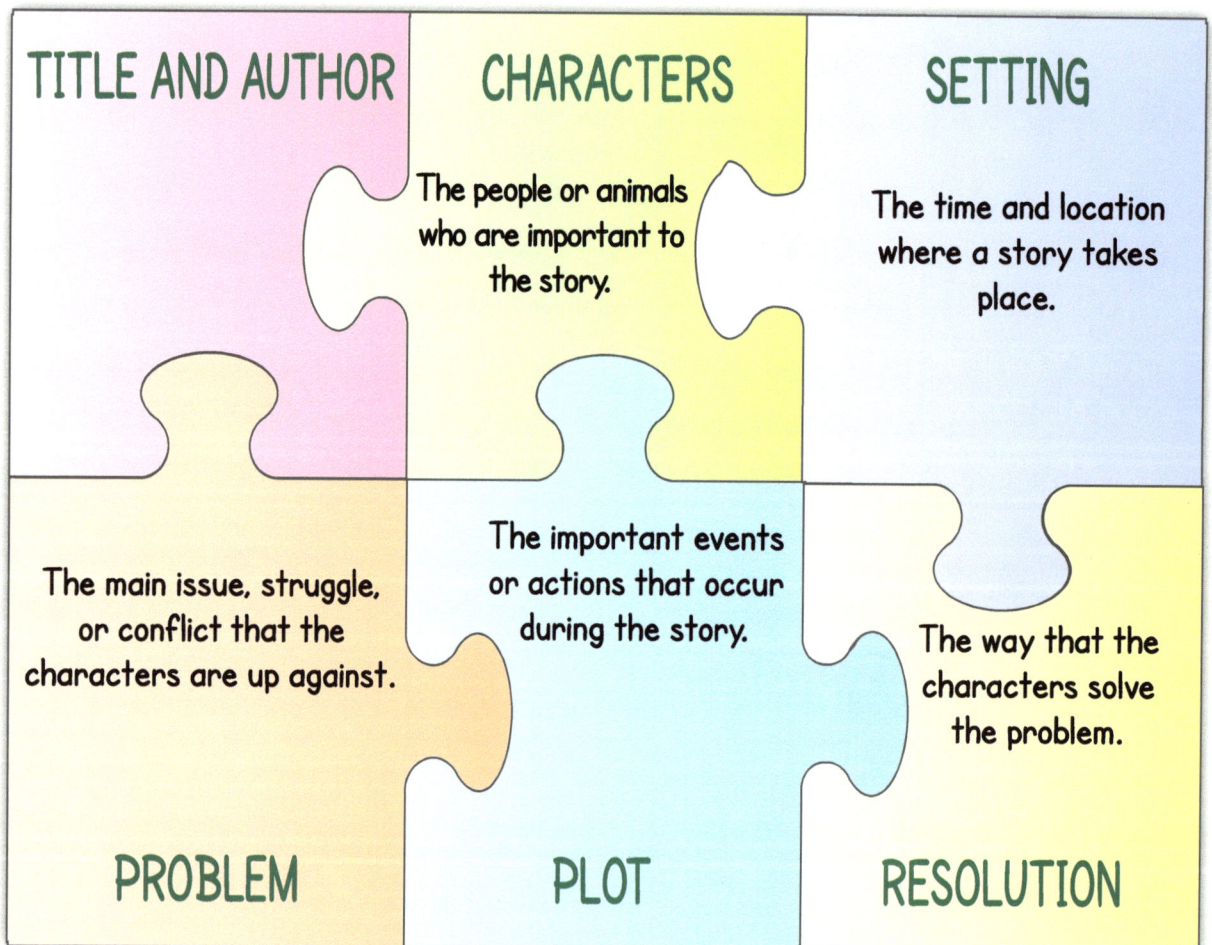

TITLE AND AUTHOR

CHARACTERS

The people or animals who are important to the story.

SETTING

The time and location where a story takes place.

The main issue, struggle, or conflict that the characters are up against.

The important events or actions that occur during the story.

The way that the characters solve the problem.

PROBLEM

PLOT

RESOLUTION

STORY MAP	
TITLE	Cinderella
SETTING	Father's and stepmother's home and the prince's castle
CHARACTERS	Cinderella, two cruel stepsisters, the fairy godmother, and the prince.
PROBLEM	The stepsisters would not allow Cinderella to accompany them to the prince's ball. Cinderella was very sad.
MAJOR EVENTS or PLOT	Her fairy godmother appeared. She changed a pumpkin into a coach with footmen, and transformed Cinderella's rags into a beautiful satin ball gown, together with diamond jewelry. In hurrying to leave the ball by midnight, Cinderella lost her glass slipper.
RESOLUTION	The Prince was sad to see Cinderella leave so quickly. He picked up her glass slipper and had his servants go throughout the land searching for its owner. Cinderella was the only person whose foot could fit into the slipper. She and the prince were married and lived happily ever after.
THEME	Cinderella teaches us that people should always strive for what they want with a kind heart and hard work.

Books to use to teach Retelling and Story Mapping

- *Little Red Riding Hood*
- *The Three Little Pigs*
- Other Fairy Tales
- *Sylvester and The Magic Pebble* by William Steig
- *Angelo* by David Macaulay
- *Arturo's Baton* by Syd Hoff
- *Grandma and the Pirates* by Phoebe Gilman

SIXTH STRATEGY – QUESTIONING

Curiosity is the greatest asset we bring to learning. The mind's desire to know more guides us to ask questions, and determine ways to find answers to those questions.

Questioning *guides the purpose* for reading, and helps us hone in on what is important. Reading with a purpose increases reading comprehension because the reader is making a personal connection with the text.

When readers ask questions as they read, they are not only *interacting with the text* to make meaning of it, but they are also *monitoring their own comprehension* of what they are reading.

- Questions move us *deeper into reading*. They stimulate thought, provide clarity, expand ideas, and lead us to further questions.
- Questioning is the *hallmark of thinking*. Proficient readers ask questions before, during and after they read.
- When readers ask questions *before they read* a text, they are activating prior knowledge, making predictions, and connecting with the text.
- Questioning *during reading* can take the form of self-questioning, questioning the text, or questioning the author. It creates a dialogue in the reader's mind as he or she reads.
- Asking questions *after reading the text* can stimulate critical analysis and further research on the topic.

Readers need to be able to differentiate between *thick and thin questions.*

- *Thin* questions are answered with factual information that can be found in the text and answered with a few words or brief sentences.
- *Thick* questions ask for opinions and ideas and require inferential thinking.

THICK AND THIN QUESTIONS

THIN QUESTIONS ?	THICK QUESTIONS ?
Can be answered easily, often with one word.	More difficult to answer.
	Need evidence to help answer questions. May be different answers to the same question
Answers are right there, in the text.	Need to think and use schema

THICK AND THIN QUESTION STARTERS

THIN QUESTIONS ?	THICK QUESTIONS ?
How many?	Why did… … … .?
Who?	How did… … … .?
When?	What do you think about… …?
Where?	What would happen if.….….?
	How would you feel if.….…?
	Why did the character do/say that… … .?

Books to use when teaching Questioning:

- *The Day of Ahmed's Secret* by Florence Parry Heide
- *Chicken Sunday* by Patricia Polacco
- *Three Questions* by John Muth
- *A Day's Work* by Eve Bunting
- *How Many Days to America* by Eve Bunting
- *Knots on a Counting Rope* by Bill Martin and John Archambault
- *The Story of Ruby Bridges* by Robert Coles
- *Sweet Clara and the Freedom Quilt* by Deborah Hopkinson

SEVENTH STRATEGY – DETERMINING IMPORTANCE

Determining Importance is a strategy that readers use to distinguish between what information in a text is ***most important*** versus what information is interesting, but not so necessary for understanding. This practical reading strategy enables students to distinguish between the most and least important information presented in all books, whether fiction or nonfiction. Determining importance allows us to move through a text coherently, to develop a line of thinking that helps our reading make sense. In order to do this, readers must sort through actions and/or information they've read and organize it as important or not so important.

For fiction, one of the best places to start is with stories that have a clear problem/solution story line. This means taking note of the characters, the setting, the problem these characters face, and the resolution to the problem.

If students cannot differentiate between important facts and not so important details, ask them:

- Is this fact part of the problem and solution?
- Is this fact part of the main idea?
- Is it really important to the outcome of the story to remember this fact?

On the other hand, for nonfiction it is important to determine the topic, the main ideas about the topic, as well as the most important details. Taking note of the vocabulary is very helpful. Readers need to filter out what is ***interesting*** from what is ***important.***

WHAT'S THE BIG IDEA?

Title: *Two Bad Ants* by Chris Van Allsburg

Important Ideas

The ants were going to find food for the queen.
They enjoyed the sugar so much that they decided to stay and eat it themselves.
After all kinds of mishaps, they made it back home.

Interesting Details

They were almost swallowed when they fell into a cup of tea.	They fell into a hot toaster.
The ants fell off the faucet into the garbage disposal.	They climbed into an electric wall outlet.

Books to use to teach Determining Importance:

- *Sylvester and the Magic Pebble* by William Steig
- *Lily's Purple Plastic Purse* by Kevin Henkes
- *The Little Engine That Could* by Watty Piper
- *Miss Rumphius* by Barbara Cooney
- *The Gardener* by Lydia Grace Finch
- *Two Bad Ants* by Chris Van Allsburg
- *Ranger Rick* – National Wildlife Federation
- *National Geographic for Kids*

EIGHTH STRATEGY – INFERRING

To make an **inference** we take information we already know, combine it with clues or facts and come up with a reasonable conclusion. Inference is a critical skill for readers to learn. So much of what we read in any kind of text is not explicitly stated, but is left for the reader to infer.

Good readers make inferences using text details and background knowledge to figure out information that isn't present in the words on the page. Making inferences helps us understand and appreciate the author's message.

It is important to make a distinction between *prediction* and *inference*.

- *Prediction* asks, "What will happen next?"
- *Inference* asks, "What conclusions can you draw from what is happening now?"

Inference is "reading between the lines."

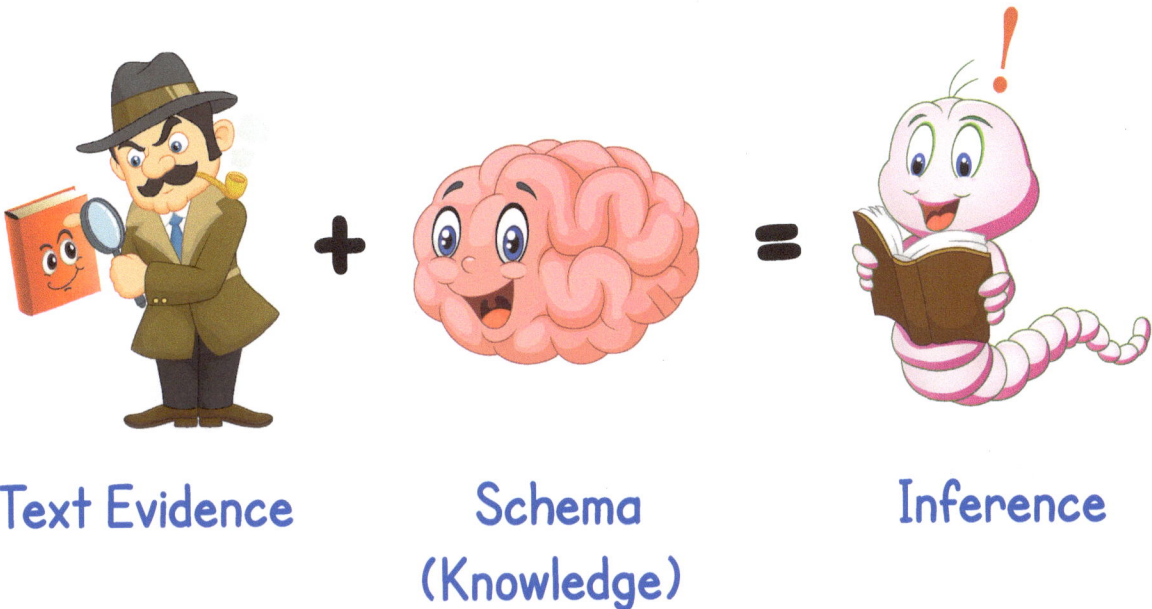

Text Evidence   **Schema (Knowledge)**   **Inference**

SUGGESTED ACTIVITIES

1. Infer from the contents in the bag what kind of family this is.

    Bring in a bag of different household items. By looking at the clues (the items in the bag), students should make educated guesses about who these items belong to. Contents include such items as make-up bottles, shaving cream, small stuffed toys, school notebook, team T-shirt, high heeled shoes, ballet slipper, nerf ball, small game like Boggle, baby formula, etc.

    Make a chart entitled Inference and Evidence.

    • Take out each item, one at a time, and have students guess what the item says about the family.
    • The "Evidence" is the item from the bag.
    • The "Inference" is what the students think the item tells about the family.
    • Students can then write three inferences they made and also draw a picture of the family.

2. Students can write or talk about the following:

    • Describe a character who is very smart, without actually saying he/she is smart.
    • Describe a very cold afternoon, without actually saying it is cold.
    • Describe an old car without actually saying the car is old.
    • Describe somewhere that is scary without actually saying it is scary.

INFERENCES

Title: *Two Bad Ants* by Chris Van Allsburg

Take information from the text	Add it to my schema	And I can infer… ….
"Then the giant scoop stirred violently back and forth. Crushing waves fell over the ants. They paddled hard to keep their tiny heads above water. But the scoop kept spinning the hot brown liquid."	From looking at the illustration, my schema tells me the spoon is stirring the liquid in a cup of tea or coffee.	Now I can infer that the ants fell into a cup of tea or coffee and are being stirred around.
"Then the lake tilted and began to empty into a cave. The ants felt themselves pulled toward the pitch black hole. Suddenly the cave disappeared and the lake became calm."	In the illustration, I see a mouth and a nose near the cup. So, I know someone is going to drink the brown liquid.	Now I can infer that the ants are in a cup, but were not drunk because the cup was put down.

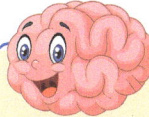

Books to teach Inference:

- *Two Bad Ants* by Chris Van Allsburg
- *The Wednesday Surprise* by Eve Bunting
- *The Rag Coat* by Lauren Mills
- *How Many Days to America* by Eve Bunting
- *Teammates* by Peter Goldenbock
- *Mary Geddy's Day* by Kate Waters
- *Mr. Lincoln's Way* by Patricia Polacco
- *Mirette on the High Wire* by Emily Arnold McCully

NINTH STRATEGY – SUMMARIZING

Summarizing teaches students how to discern the most important ideas in a text, how to ignore irrelevant information, and how to integrate the central ideas in a meaningful way.

It teaches students how to take a large selection of text and reduce it to the main points for more concise understanding. When you summarize something, you write or tell the general idea and only the *most important points*. Do not include your own opinion.

The difference between summarizing and retelling is:

- A **summary** is direct and to the point. It is like a postcard of a vacation.
- A **retelling** is the entire scrapbook. It provides as many details as possible and is usually an oral activity.

There is a difference between a fiction and nonfiction summary.

In a **fiction summary**, you focus on the characters, the events, the problem and the solution.

An easy way to introduce **summarizing fiction** to students is to use these basic signal words:

Someone…… Wanted…… But…… So……Then………

In a **nonfiction summary** you focus on the important details and facts, that help you create a main idea. There are five main components of a nonfiction summary:

Who? What? When? Where? Why?

ORGANIZER FOR SUMMARIZING FICTION

Title: *The Big Bad Wolf and The Three Little Pigs.*

SOMEONE – Who is the main character?

The Big Bad Wolf

WANTED – What did this character want?

To eat the Three Little Pigs

BUT – What was the problem?

He could not blow the brick house down

SO – How did the character try to solve the problem?

He came down the chimney and fell into a pot of boiling water.

THEN – What was the resolution to the problem?

The Three Little Pigs celebrated.

Now that you have organized your information, it is easy to write a 3-5 line summary:

The big, bad wolf wanted to eat the pigs for dinner. He could not blow the pig's brick house down, so he came down the chimney and fell into a pot of boiling water. The pigs celebrated their victory and their survival.

ORGANIZER FOR SUMMARIZING NONFICTION

BOOK TITLE

A Picture Book of Frederick Douglass by David Adler

WHO is the most important subject?

Frederick Douglass

WHAT did he/she do?

Helped lead struggle to end slavery. Worked for equal rights.

WHEN did this take place?

1800 to 1890

WHERE did this happen?

Southeastern and Northeastern United States

WHY is the subject important?

His writings, speeches, actions, and example changed people's views of African-Americans, and helped lead to the conclusion that all people are equal.

Now that you have organized your information, it is easy to write a 3-5 line summary:

Frederick Douglass, born a slave, who lived from 1800 to 1890, helped lead the struggle to end slavery in the Southeastern and Northeastern United States. In writings, speeches, actions, and by example, he changed people's views of African-Americas, helping lead to the conclusion that all people are equal.

Books to use to teach Summarizing:

Fiction:

- Fairy Tales
- *Cloudy with a Chance of Meatballs* by Judi Barrett
- *Jumanji* by Chris Van Allsburg
- *The Librarian of Basra* by Jeanette Winter
- *Weslandia* by Paul Fleishman
- *Miss Rumphius* by Barbara Cooney
- *Just Plain Fancy* by Patricia Polacco

Nonfiction:

- *The Man Who Walked Between the Towers* by Mordechai Gerstein
- *My Name is Georgia* by Jeanette Winter
- *Malala, A Brave Girl from Pakistan* by Jeanette Winter
- *A Picture Book of Frederick Douglass* by David Adler
- *Nasreen's Secret School: A True Story from Afghanistan* by Jeanette Winter

TENTH STRATEGY – MONITORING AND CLARIFYING

Good readers use their inner voice to think about what they are reading

The Monitoring/Clarifying strategy teaches students to recognize when they don't understand parts of a text, and to take necessary steps to restore meaning.

- We *monitor* our comprehension when we focus on making sure we understand what we are reading.
- We *clarify* our comprehension to find our why we have not understood, and then use specific strategies to figure out the meaning of what we are reading.

Examples of Fix-up Strategies

If the meaning of the text is not clear to the reader:

- Stop and think about what you have read
- Adjust the reading rate
- Re-read the sections that do not make sense (silently or out loud)
- Look up unfamiliar words or terms
- Look at the pictures, charts, or diagrams for clues
- Look at the key words, bold print, italicized words and punctuation
- Keep on reading for context clues
- Make mental images in your mind – Visualize
- Search for headings that may provide clarification
- Try to connect the text to something you have read in another book, what you know about the world, or to something you have experienced.

GOOD READERS
Back up and Reread
when something doesn't make sense while reading.

MONITOR AND CLARIFY

Title: *Rechenka's Eggs* by Patricia Polacco

Monitor What I do not understand, and page number	Clarify Which fix-up strategy I used	I understand… … now I can keep on reading
P.1 dacha	I read ahead and came across the meaning.	yes
P.6 "As they glided over the snow, one of them faltered and fell from the sky."	I made a mental picture in my mind to fully understand what was happening.	yes
P.18 Onion Domes	I looked at the illustrations to see what they are.	yes

Books to use to teach Monitoring for Meaning and Clarifying

- *Chester's Way* by Kevin Henkes
- *The Stories Julian Tells* by Ann Cameron
- *The Gardener* by Sarah Stewart
- *The Wise Woman and Her Secret* by Eve Merriam
- *The Honest-to-Goodness Truth* by Patricia McKissack

ELEVENTH STRATEGY – THEME

Identifying the theme of a story is a higher-order thinking skill and requires the reader to make an inference.

THEME is "The Big Picture." It is what the author wants you to learn or know.

- It is **NOT** the events or the characters, time, place, setting or plot.
- It is **NOT** the topic of the story.

It is important to differentiate between the Theme and the Main Idea of a story.

The ***Main idea*** is what the story is all about.

The ***Theme*** is the underlying message which the author wishes to convey to the reader.

- It is what the story teaches the reader.
- The *theme* is bigger than the story.
- It is rarely stated in the text.
- Instead, the reader must consider how characters respond to challenges, or how the narrator reflects upon a topic to infer the theme.

It is helpful for students who are trying to come up with the theme of a story to ask them:

- *What did the author want us to think about?*
- *What idea stays with you?*
- *What will you remember about this story?*
- *What did the author want us to learn from the story?*

Teaching theme gets at the heart of what we want for students—authentic, meaningful, and memorable experiences with the text.

COMMON THEMES FOUND IN LITERATURE

Many books contain a theme or a message from the author.

Acceptance	These books have characters who accept and respect others' differences and beliefs.
Courage	These books have brave characters who have the strength to overcome a fear or accept a risk.
Perseverance	These books have characters who never give up, even when facing difficult times.
Cooperation	These books have characters who work together to solve a problem or achieve a goal.
Compassion	These books have characters who want to make those who are suffering feel better.
Honesty	These books have characters who find it is always best to tell the truth.
Kindness	These books have friendly characters who are generous and considerate of others.
Loyalty	These books have characters who trust each other and never turn their backs on their friends.
Gratitude	These books have characters who, despite what has happened in the story, are grateful and appreciative for what they have.
Bullying	These books have characters who purposefully hurt others by their mean words or actions.

Books to use to teach Theme:

- Fables
- Fairy Tales
- *Salt in His Shoes: Michael Jordan in Pursuit of a Dream* by Deloris Jordan
- *Oliver Button is a Sissy* by Tomie de Paola
- *Those shoes* by Maribeth Boelts
- *The Invisible Boy* by Trudy Ludwig
- *The Hungry Coat* by Demi
- *Mr. Peabody's Apples* by Madonna
- *A Day's Work* by Eve Bunting

TWELFTH STRATEGY – SYNTHESIS

What you know **+** What you have just read **=** SYNTHESIS

Synthesizing

Put the Pieces Together

It is important to differentiate between summarizing and synthesizing

- When we *summarize* we pick the most important things that we have just read and write them in just a few sentences.

- When we *synthesize*, we pull together the most important points from our reading, but we move beyond what's stated by the author.

The prefix "syn" means together. Synthesizing is combining new ideas with what we already know, to get something new and different. We access our schema - our prior knowledge - and then add our understanding of what we've read to create a new understanding of what we are reading. Our thinking expands as we read.

A good analogy is to explain to students that synthesizing is similar to making a chicken stew. We start with chicken. Then we add vegetables and spices. We combine all the necessary individual ingredients and mix them up to make something new – a delicious chicken stew. When we **synthesize,** we take what we already know and mix it with what we have learned from reading to create new ideas and understandings.

As students read, encourage them to use these phrases to synthesize the information:

- When I started reading I thought…
- Now I understand that…
- I am changing my mind about…
- This gives me an idea…
- That leads me to believe…
- Now this changes everything…
- My opinion now is…

Synthesizing

Put the Pieces
Together

SYNTHESIS IS WHEN YOU ADD NEW INFORMATION TO YOUR EXISTING SCHEMA, AND YOUR THINKING CHANGES

Title of the Book: *The Fox and the Crow* - A Fable
Author: Aesop

As you read your book, record what you are thinking.

AT FIRST I WAS THINKING … … … This story was going to be about a group of crows.

THEN I BEGAN TO THINK … … … It was going to be about just one young, very vain crow, who was only interested in how handsome he or she was.

NOW I THINK … … … It is about how vanity leads to a fall, because the smart fox was able to charm the crow out of his or her piece of meat.

Books to use to teach Synthesizing

- Fables are a useful genre for introducing synthesizing because of their short structure and straightforward messages.
- *Smoky Night* by Eve Bunting
- *Henry's Freedom Box* by Ellen Levine
- *The Polar Express* by Chris Van Allsburg
- *Under the Quilt of Night* by Deborah Hopkinson
- *The Summer My Father Was Ten* by Pat Brisson
- *Granddaddy's Gift* by Margaree King Mitchell
- *Goin' Someplace Special* by Patricia McKissack

APPENDIX

WAYS TO HELP YOUR CHILD

Reading is best done in a quiet and comfortable place. Make reading a relaxed, stress-free time with your child. Let your child see you reading. Read aloud to your child; reread favorite stories. Discuss stories you read together. One of the best things you can do to assist your child with reading is to talk about the books or articles they read. Talking stimulates language development and helps children improve their comprehension – their understanding of what they read. Retelling a story or even a chapter is an ideal vehicle for students to delve deeply into their own understanding, merging their knowledge of the world with the meaning they derived from what they've just read. When children realize that thoughtful discussion is encouraged and appreciated after reading, they will begin to apply that level of thinking themselves. They will expect that the texts they are reading will make sense and that it is their responsibility to process the meaning.

A first step might be a "**before reading**" conversation: talk about the cover, the title, the table of contents, and a few of the pictures in the book. Mostly, try to help your child connect personal experiences to the reading. For example, if the story is about a place far from home, the two of you can share an experience you had when you went on vacation.

During the time your child is reading, invite your child to talk about the book. The question, "What do you think might happen next?" is always a good lead. Children love to share their opinions.

After the reading, you might start with questions such as:

"What did you notice?"

"What did you like?"

"How did it make you feel?"

"Did this remind you of any experiences you have had?"

"What parts of the story were your favorites?

SUPPORTIVE PRAISE

The most important thing is to stay positive and supportive.

a. "I like the way you worked that out. Good for you."

b. "Yes, that word would make sense."

c. "That was a good try."

d. "You're trying it again and not getting frustrated. That's great!"

e. "I like the way you looked at that picture to help yourself."

f. "You went back to the beginning of the sentence and tried it again. That's what good readers do."

g. "You didn't give up."

h. "You are getting better every day."

i. "You're really becoming a good reader. I'm proud of you."

STUDENT RESPONSE SHEETS FOR THE STRATEGIES

PRE-READING CHART

Browsing through text prior to reading it can help students activate their schema (prior knowledge) and set a purpose for reading. Examining the content and format of the text helps them understand what they will be reading, become aware of the text layout, and activate any schema they may have on the topic.

Title of the Book: _

Author: _

TEXT	MY RESPONSE
Read the title and look at the picture on the cover. What do you think the book will be about?	
Is this fiction of nonfiction?	
If this is fiction, what can you tell about the characters, setting or plot? If this is nonfiction, what is the main topic? What do you think you may learn from reading this book?	
Does this book remind you of any other books you've read? If so, what books? What in the text reminds you of it?	
Are you interested in reading this book? Why?	

CONCEPT WEB

Text to Self

TEXT-TO-SELF CONNECTIONS CHART

Title of the Book: _

Author: _

If you read something in the text that you can connect to your own life, make a note of it. Copy it below and explain your connection.

MY TEXT-TO-SELF CONNECTION Picture or a quote from the text	This reminds me of and helped me understand… … …

Text to Text

TEXT-TO-TEXT CONNECTIONS CHART

Title of the Book: _

Author: _

If you read something in your text that reminds you of something else you have read in another book or article or other piece of writing, make a note of it. Copy it below and explain your connection.

MY TEXT-TO-TEXT CONNECTION Picture or a quote from the text	This reminds me of and helped me understand… … …

Text to World   TEXT-TO-WORLD CONNECTIONS CHART

Title of the Book: _

Author: _

If you read something in your text and it reminds you of something happening in the outside world, make a note of it. It may be a news event or social issue. Copy it below and explain your connection.

MY TEXT-TO-WORLD CONNECTION Picture or a quote from the text	This reminds me of and helped me understand… … …

PREDICTIONS

Draw a picture or write what you think will happen next	What clues did you use for your predictions?

REMEMBER: It is just fine if your prediction did not come true.
The important thing is that your prediction makes sense with what you have read.

VISUALIZING

Write down powerful sentences or phrases from the text that helped you visualize. Sketch what you visualized on the other side.

These Words	Created This Image

F.A.S.T
FEELINGS - ACTIONS - SAYINGS - THOUGHTS

In the boxes below, describe the
Feelings, Actions, Sayings and Thoughts of your character.

Title of the Book: _____

Character's Name: _____

FEELINGS	ACTIONS

SAYINGS	THOUGHTS

INSIDE/OUTSIDE CHARACTER TRAIT

Title of the Book: _____

Author: _____

Character's Name:_____

OUTSIDE: Appearance What does the character look like on the outside?	INSIDE: Character Traits What is the character like on the inside?

CHARACTER MAP

Title of the Book: _

Author: _

How the Character Acts and Feels.	How Others Think About this Character.

Character's Name

_ _ _ _ _ _ _ _ _ _ _ _ _ _ _ _ _ _ _ _

Describe the Character's Outward Appearance.	What Does the Character Like or Dislike?

RETELLING GUIDE

The title of the story is . . .	
The characters are . . .	
The story takes place . . .	
In the beginning . . .	
Then . . .	
After that . . .	
And then . . .	
Then . . .	
In the end . . .	

STORY ELEMENTS

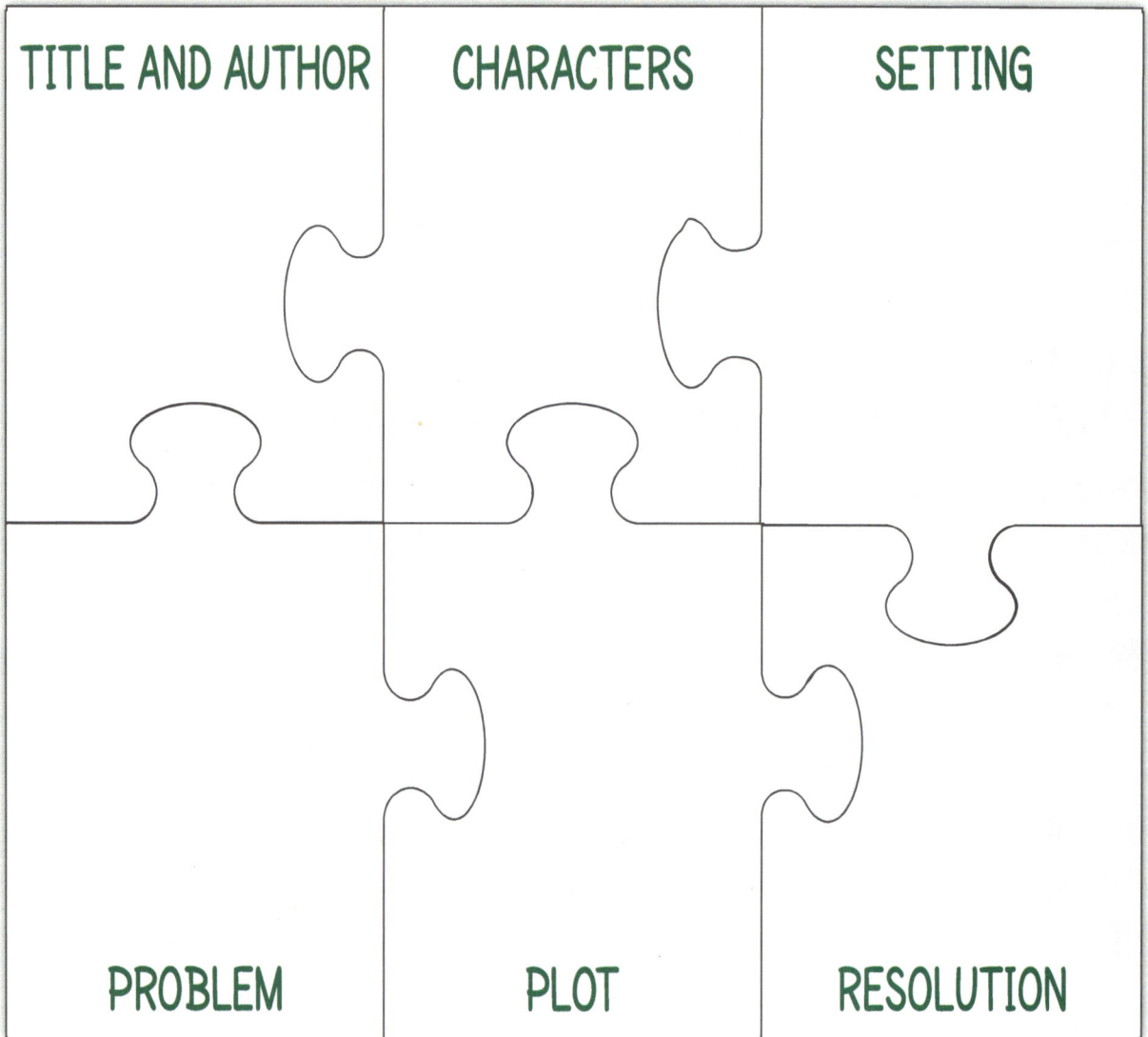

TITLE AND AUTHOR	CHARACTERS	SETTING
PROBLEM	PLOT	RESOLUTION

STORY MAP

TITLE	
SETTING	
CHARACTERS	
PROBLEM	
MAJOR EVENTS or PLOT	
RESOLUTION	
THEME	

WHAT'S THE BIG IDEA?

Title of the Book: _____

Important Ideas

Interesting Details

INFERENCES

Title of the Book: _____

Take information from the text	Add it to my schema	And I can infer… ….

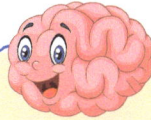

ORGANIZER FOR SUMMARIZING FICTION

Title of the Book: _

SOMEONE—Who is the main character?

WANTED—What did this character want?

BUT—What was the problem?

SO—How did the character try to solve the problem?

THEN—What was the resolution to the problem?

Now that you have organized your information, it is easy to write a 3-5 line summary:

ORGANIZER FOR SUMMARIZING NONFICTION

BOOK TITLE

WHO is the most important subject?

WHAT did he/she do?

WHEN did this take place?

WHERE did this happen?

WHY is the subject important?

Now that you have organized your information, it is easy to write a 3-5 line summary:

GOOD READERS
Back up and Reread
when something doesn't
make sense while reading.

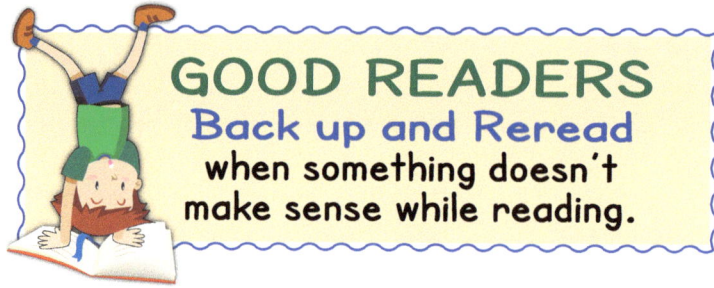

MONITOR AND CLARIFY

Title of the Book: _ _ _ _ _ _ _ _ _ _ _ _ _ _ _ _ _ _ _

Monitor	Clarify	I understand… …
What I do not understand, and page number	Which fix-up strategy I used	now I can keep on reading

Synthesizing
Put the Pieces Together

SYNTHESIS IS WHEN YOU ADD NEW INFORMATION TO YOUR EXISTING SCHEMA, AND YOUR THINKING CHANGES

Title of the Book: _

Author: _

As you read your book, record what you are thinking.

AT FIRST I WAS THINKING … … …

THEN I BEGAN TO THINK … … …

NOW I THINK … … …

GENRE

Books can be divided into two main groups: they are either **fiction** or **nonfiction**.

Nonfiction books contain real or factual information and are meant to inform the reader about the real world. Fiction contains stories made up by the author, and are meant to entertain the reader. These two types of books can then be divided into categories which are called *genres*. *Genre* is a French word meaning "a type, or a kind." Exposure to texts from a wide variety of genres opens up new worlds to read.

FICTION

GENRE	FEATURES
Realistic fiction	This is a made-up story which is true to life.
Fantasy	A made-up story that does not happen in real life. May have magic and talking animals.
Mystery	These stories involve crimes. Clues are provided for the reader.
Science Fiction	These stories often involve time travel, fantasy and speculation.
Historical Fiction	A story based on real events from the past, set during a particular historical time period.
Fables, Folk Tales, Fairy Tales	Stories that have been passed down from generation to generation, usually by word of mouth, often with a moral.

NONFICTION

GENRE	FEATURES
Biography	Story of someone's life told by another person.
Autobiography	Story of someone's life told by that person.
Informational Text	Written to specifically inform the reader about a particular subject.

NONFICTION TEXT FEATURES

Nonfiction Text Features are the features that help a reader to navigate a Nonfiction Text more easily. Text features include all the components of a story or article that are not the main body of text.

Common Text Features

Name of text feature	Purpose of text feature
Title	Quickly tells the reader what information they will learn.
Table of contents	Shows students the different chapter or section titles and where they are located.
Index	Directs students where to go in the text to find specific information on a topic, word, or person. The words are listed in alphabetical order.
Glossary	Identifies important vocabulary words for students and gives their definitions.
Headings or subtitles	Help the reader identify the main idea for that section of text. It is written in larger, bold print.
Sidebars	Are set apart from the main text, (usually located on the side or bottom of the page) and elaborate on a detail mentioned in the text.
Pictures and captions	Show an important object or idea from the text.
Labeled diagrams	A drawing or a picture with labels.
Charts and graphs	Visual aids used to compare and contrast information from the text.
Maps	Help a reader locate a place in the world that is related to text.

Text Features are used to help a reader better understand nonfiction texts!

Using Nonfiction Text Features

Name of text feature	Title and Page	How this helped me…
Title		
Table of contents		
Photo/Illustration		
Diagram		
Chart/Graph		
Caption		
Map		
Index		

OMNI Learning Center Educational Guides

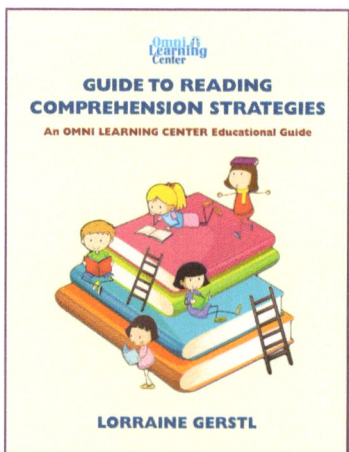

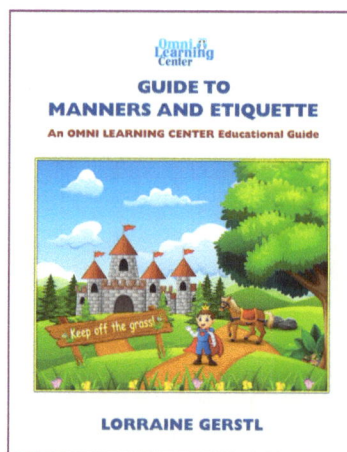

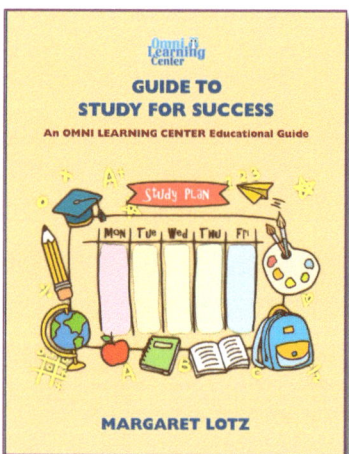

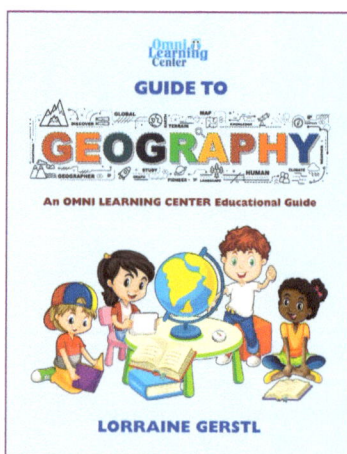

Available Now!

GUIDE TO READING COMPREHENSION STRATEGIES
An OMNI LEARNING CENTER Educational Guide

LORRAINE GERSTL

GUIDE TO MANNERS AND ETIQUETTE
An OMNI LEARNING CENTER Educational Guide

Keep off the grass!

LORRAINE GERSTL

GUIDE TO STUDY FOR SUCCESS
An OMNI LEARNING CENTER Educational Guide

Study Plan

MON TUE WED THU FRI

MARGARET LOTZ

GUIDE TO GEOGRAPHY
An OMNI LEARNING CENTER Educational Guide

LORRAINE GERSTL

The books are available at special quantity discounts for bulk purchase.
For details, write to: *sales@OmniLearningCenter.org*

Omni Learning Center

25579 Carmel Knolls Drive, Carmel - CA, 93923
Telephone: 831-277-3387 / 831-224-0742
contact@OmniLearningCenter.org
www.OmniLearningCenter.org

www.ingramcontent.com/pod-product-compliance
Lightning Source LLC
Chambersburg PA
CBHW061353090426

42739CB00002B/16